W9-AHT-237

To

From

Date

I am fearfully and wonderfully made.
Psalm 139:14

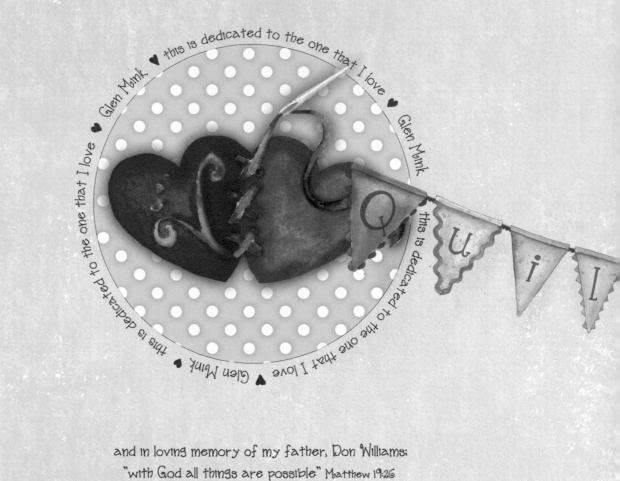

Glen Mink ♥ this is dedicated to the one that I love ♥ Glen Mink this is dedicated to the one that I love ♥ Glen Mink ♥ this is dedicated to the one that I love

Quil

and in loving memory of my father, Don Williams;
"with God all things are possible" Matthew 19:26

Every Quilt Has a Story

Written & Illustrated by

Nancy E. Mink

HARVEST HOUSE PUBLISHERS
EUGENE, OREGON

Every Quilt Has a Story

Text and artwork copyright ©2013 by Nancy E. Mink

Published by Harvest House Publishers
Eugene, Oregon 97402
www.harvesthousepublishers.com

ISBN 978-0-7369-5205-7

Design and production by Dugan Design Group,
Bloomington, Minnesota

Harvest House Publishers has made every effort to trace the ownership
of all poems and quotes. In the event of a question arising from the use
of a poem or quote, we regret any error made and will be pleased to
make the necessary correction in future editions of this book.

All Scriptures are taken from the Holy Bible, New International
Version®, NIV®. Copyright © 1973, 1978, 1984, 2011, by Biblica,
Inc.™ Used by permission of Zondervan. All rights reserved worldwide.
www.zondervan.com

Table of Contents

Every Quilt Has

QUILT:
Three layers of fabric sewn (quilted)
together to form a homogeneous blanket or
textile work of art: a top layer for design, middle
layer of filling (batting), and bottom layer of
coordinating fabric (backing).

Quilts were draped over every available time-worn porch railing while
hundreds more swung on ropes tied between towering ponderosa pines.
With the help of a cool mountain breeze, they gently waved to me as my
husband and I drove through the quaint—and on this day, most
colorful—gold rush town. I succumbed to their
beckoning as if they said, "Come closer. See our beauty
and hear our stories."

Unbeknownst to me, the local guild was
holding an international quilt show,

4

Story

and I was captivated by the tapestry of colors, elaborate fabric piecing, and, oh, the intricate stitching! Each quilt had a card pinned to the back of it, which explained the what, where, when, why, and who of its little quilt life.

Stumbling upon that big show in that charming small town started my love affair with quilts that has grown through the decades. I can't pass up a quilt, whether it's in someone's home, at a show, or in a thrift shop without my imagination wondering about its story. *What brought you here, my precious?*

Locked inside the stitches of every quilt are bits and pieces of life. Celebrations and adventures, hopes, and dreams, even hardships and sorrows are sewn between the layers.

Whether you quilt or are just fond of quilts, relax and delight in these heartwarming stories, quotes, and poems of love and love lost, happiness and sorrow, and most of all, friends among quilts

> Locked inside the stitches of every quilt are bits and pieces of life.

Crossing Borders

BORDER:
Fabric sewn around the quilt to frame and enhance the design.

The road to a friend's house is never long.

Linda French is a contemporary quilt artist and instructor from Centerville, Ohio, who sews most of her award-winning quilts in her "Florida Room." Inspired by the view of her peaceful gardens, she uses elaborate stitches to create warm, cheerful quilts from intricately pieced fabrics.

A few decades ago, however, Linda's life was not as settled as it is today. After her husband accepted a job offer and they moved across a country, over an ocean, and to the land down under, Australia became their new home. With a toddler in tow, adjusting to the new life took effort and lots of planning. Priorities had to be set. And what was at the top of Linda's list? Quilting, of course! By the end of her first week in Australia, Linda had attended a quilt guild meeting and met Susan, who offered Linda assistance with whatever she needed to get settled.

"A few days later, my daughter was sick, and I gave Susan a call. That began a friendship we both cherish. When I left Australia to go back to the States, leaving Susan was the hardest part."

When twilight drops her curtain down
And pins it with a star.
Remember that you have a friend
Though she may wander far.

-Lucy Maud Montgomery,
from *Anne of Green Gables*

Ten years passed before they could meet face-to-face again. They attended a quilt show in Paducah, Kentucky, together and visited as old friends do. As the years passed, toddlers grew up, new homes were established, lifetime occupations were retired, and award-winning quilts were quilted.

It's been almost thirty years since that first quilt guild meeting, yet Linda and Susan remain long-distance companions. When asked how they've kept their friendship strong, Linda responds simply, "We keep in touch!"

When I asked Linda if she had a favorite quilt, she mentioned that her Circles of Life quilt would have to be at the top of the list. From the first to the last quilted stitch, Linda enjoyed the sewing process more than displaying the finished quilt at any show. Yet, show it she did! The quilt has won ten first-place and best-of-show awards. Although it's hard to imagine, this one was the first quilt she had ever entered in a show.

In such a fast-paced, hurry-up world, it's refreshing to hear a busy person with so many accolades talk about taking time to enjoy the journey instead of focusing on the destination. How true that is of all life's meaningful things. Much like intricately quilting her "undulating feathers" and "French sweethearts," relationships take time, patience, and love. Friendship's sweet journey endures a few sour bumps on the way to the delicious reward of faithful companionship.

Linda's advice to beginning quilters so aptly applies to friendship and other matters of significance: "We are sewers and quilters because we enjoy it. Don't be in such a hurry to finish. Play a lot, make changes as you go, and you will like the end result more."

Tea pot is on, the cups are waiting,
Favorite chairs anticipating.
No matter what I have to do,
My friend, there's always time for you.

Author Unknown

May our paths always lead us back to one another.

7

Patchwork of Perfection

PATCHWORK:
An older term for sewing various pieces of cut fabric together to form a lovely design or quilt block.

Near the end of His ministry, Jesus told His disciples in John 15:15, "I no longer call you servants, because a servant does not know his master's business. Instead, I have called you friends, for everything that I have learned from my Father I have made known to you."

We strive to be good servants because we think that it's God's highest calling. Yet this verse regards friendship as a step higher. In the old hymn, we sing, "What a friend we have in Jesus, all our sins and grief to bear." *Am I a good servant to Him? Am I a good friend?*

Friendship involves acceptance, understanding, trust, and respect. Making and keeping a friend takes time. Meeting people through social networking and instant electronic communication gizmos is easy, yet long-lasting, loving friendships require more than a click of a button. There is no substitute for a live, face-to-face friend.

Joining a group that shares your passion for quilting, cooking, gardening, or a sport is a good start toward making friends. Quilters are especially blessed. Quilt guilds have become popular and are springing up in even the smallest towns. If your local fabric shop doesn't have one, chances are they would like to start one.

If You Had a Friend

If you had a friend strong, simple, true,
Who knew your faults and who understood;
Who believed in the very best of you,
And who cared for you as a father would;
Who would stick by you to the very end,
Who would smile however the world might frown:
I'm sure you would try to please your friend,
You never would think to throw him down.

And supposing your friend was high and great,
And he lived in a palace rich and tall,
And sat like a King in shining state,
And his praise was loud on the lips of all;
Well then, when he turned to you alone,
And he singled you out from all the crowd,
And he called you up to his golden throne,
Oh, wouldn't you just be jolly proud?

If you had a friend like this, I say,
So sweet and tender, so strong and true,
You'd try to please him in every way,
You'd live at your bravest—now, wouldn't you?
His worth would shine in the words you penned;
You'd shout his praises…yet now it's odd!
You tell me you haven't got such a friend;
You haven't? I wonder… What of God?

Robert William Service

9

Friends Among Quilts

QUILT GUILD:
An organized group
of people who meet to
learn about and advance
the art of quilting and
textile arts.

Happy talk could be heard from the doorway as it rippled over bolts of calico and gingham. It mingled with laughter as it swirled around spools of thread and fanciful quilt pattern books until it finally ended its course at my ears. "It was chompin' on the winery's prize-winning grapes!" the unidentified voice wailed. I chuckled at the story of how to retrieve a llama from a vineyard.

The stream of amusement coming from the backroom quilting bee kept me entertained while I decided on which hue—blush rose or coral pink—I would need for the border of my new Lone Star quilt. As I listened, I was reminded of one of the main reasons we quilt. Friendship! Quilting brings people together to forge new friendships and strengthen old ones.

Friendship is born at that moment
when one person says to another:
"What! You too? I thought I
was the only one."

C.S. Lewis

Although people join quilt guilds for different reasons, many join to meet new friends and learn more about quilting. Other fun benefits include the opportunity to:

- Meet professional quilters, quilt shop owners, authors, pattern designers, and quilters from different cultures and backgrounds
- Participate in social activities outside the guild meetings
- Learn new block patterns by exchanging quilt blocks and making friendship quilts
- Donate to charity projects by helping to sew handmade guild quilts to

give to children's homes, veterans' organizations, and women's shelters

- Take part in quilt shows
- Receive training via speakers, workshops, and guild library books, which are often purchased through guild fund-raisers

A gift made by hand is a gift from the heart

A good friend, like a treasured quilt, ages with you and never loses its warmth.

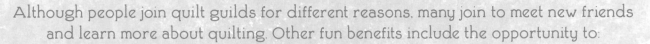

II

Ties That Bind

BINDING:
Strips of fabric sewn over the raw
edges of a quilt to add strength and
a finished look.

The best thing to spend on a friend is time. Gestures and little gifts between friends help bind us together. A handwritten card, a just-because-I-love-you tea, or a thoughtful, homemade gift shows you care. Abundant blessings flow from nurtured friendships.

The "friendship quilt" fad spread throughout young America in the 1840s. Typically relatives and friends quickly pieced fabric scraps to make individual quilt blocks, signed their work by either embroidering their name or writing it with indelible ink, and then stitched the blocks together to create the quilt. No matter their economic circumstance, most women could collect enough scrap fabric to make a block to add to the quilt.

The westward expansion furthered the importance of this quilt design. Pioneer women received only occasional letters to connect them with family and friends, so the friendship quilt became a precious keepsake to remind them of loved ones living far away or those lost to illness and war.

Sampler album quilts, popular during the Victorian era, were also a form of tribute or commemoration. Instead of using fabric scraps, women pieced or appliqued the quilt blocks from stylish fabric, signed them elegantly, and included small drawings and verses.

Today the tradition continues as friends gather to sew, sign, and quilt blocks of similar sizes to commemorate a retirement, honor a birthday, celebrate a wedding, or comfort a loved one recovering from an illness.

12

A friend knows
the song in your heart
and sings it back to you.

Author Unknown

13

And then while you're livin' your life, it looks pretty much like a jumble o'
quilt pieces before they're put together; but when you git through with it, or pretty nigh through,
as I am now, you'll see the use and purpose of everything in it. Everything'll be in its right place
jest like the squares in this "four-patch," and one piece may be pretty and another one ugly, but it
all looks right when you see it finished and joined together.

Eliza Calvert Hall, from *Aunt Jane of Kentucky*

Ways to Sign a Quilt Block

Stabilize the signature area by ironing freezer paper to the back side of the fabric and then choose one of the following ways to add a signature:

- Handwrite your signature using a pen with permanent, waterproof ink or a fabric pen.

- Stamp your signature or message using a deeply etched rubber stamp coated with colorfast, fabric-safe ink.

- Embroider your signature onto the fabric by using your handwritten signature as a pattern.

- Print your signature onto premade sheets of computer printer fabric (available at large fabric shops and online) using your computer and a waterproof ink cartridge.

Note: Test all methods before applying and when finished, set with a dry, warm iron.

Barn Quilts

European immigrants started painting quilt squares on barns in America more than 300 years ago. In some states communities are reviving the art form by again painting quilts onto the sides of beautiful, historic barns. They then print maps to the various locations and call it a "Barn Quilt Trail," inspiring quilt lovers far and wide.

Secrets in the Calico

CALICO:
A plain, woven cotton cloth
printed with colorful, small,
repeating designs.

Touch a quilt, and you touch a part of the maker's soul. With calicos faded from time and wear, edges frayed and stitches lost, the old quilt becomes more precious with time because of the memories preserved within the layers of fabric.

Tender stories of hopes, dreams, courage, and even frustrations have been torn from diaries and letters or printed on a bit of fabric and tacked to the back of a few older quilts. Although most of these stories were meant to be private, some quilts have survived many generations and now reveal important history.

Most quilts, however, are never documented, and our imagination is left to fill in the story of why the pattern and fabric were chosen, who or what the quilt was made for, and most of all, who spent part of their life making it.

No matter how commonplace you feel your project is, it needs a label. It should, at the least, show who, when, where, and why the quilt was made. You might also include interesting information unique to the maker and quilt, such as the quilt name, pattern, size, who pieced the top, who quilted it, and the date it was started and finished. Even pictures are sometimes printed on labels.

Quilting has made a big comeback. An estimated 21 million active American quilters collectively spend more than 2 billion a year on their passion. What stories will their quilts tell future generations?

As lonely through this world I stray,

And pass the pensive hours;

May truth and virtue point the way

And strew my path with flowers.

M.E. Peach, an inscription on a quilt from 1850

Accept my friend this little pledge

Your love and friendship to engage

If ere we should be called to part

Let this be settled in your heart

That when this little piece you see

You ever will remember me.

Zachariah Allen,
an inscription on a friendship
quilt from the 1860s

I made quilts as fast as I could to keep
my family warm, and as pretty as I
could to keep my heart from breaking.

From a pioneer woman's diary

17

Facing the Challenge

QUILT CHALLENGE:
A competition to create quilt blocks using specified fabrics or piecework patterns.

Pioneer quilts were sewn to fulfill a basic need. While men talked of migrating west to stake claims for rich and plentiful farmland, the women worried about the challenges and dangers they would face. Friendship quilts represented cozy scrapbooks of friends and family who were left behind.

Quilts were a staple on the wagon trail. Not only used for bedding, quilts padded wagon seats, covered cracks during choking dust storms, protected against Indian attacks, divided the small wagon and provided privacy, and sometimes substituted for a burial cloth. If the pioneer woman was lucky, her prized friendship quilt was intact at the end of the journey—tucked safely in a trunk, wrapped carefully around her breakables.

How lucky I am
to have something that
makes saying goodbye
so hard.

A.A. Milne,
from *Winnie-the-Pooh*

19

A Growing Friendship Album

ALBUM QUILT:
A quilt made of different blocks that friends or family sign.

Every now and then you come across a real-life fairy tale. Once upon a time, two pretty little girls named Sarah and Rebecca met each other in kindergarten. They became close friends in elementary school and best friends in middle school. In high school and college, they were inseparable.

In class one day, Sarah made Rebecca a silly little flower from construction paper and wrote these words on it: "To Rebecca—Love for always, Sarah." Sarah then glued the flower into a plastic butter tub, wrote the words "My love for you grows," on the long stem and gave it to Rebecca.

Eventually Sarah met a boy, as did Rebecca. In turn each girl took her place beside the other as a maid of honor, laughing, crying, and helping with the day's important events. Although Rebecca and Sarah started their families separately, they both thought they'd have three boys.

When God added a cute little girl to Rebecca's family, Sarah Johnson—now a quilter, designer, and blogger—made a darling quilt from pretty calicos and a line of whimsical prints named, "My Love Grows and Grows," reminiscent of that long-ago paper-flower gift. "When I saw the design of this quilt, I knew this had to be a quilt for her," said Sarah. "I thank God for a friend who knows me better than anyone else, who has been through good times and bad, and will be there…for always! And can you believe that when I gave Rebecca this quilt, she pulled out the flower that I had made for her almost seventeen years ago? The red petals of the flower have faded and now they match the peach colors in the quilt almost perfectly. We are truly blessed to have each other!"

Once in a while
right in the middle of life
LOVE gives us a
fairy tale.

Author Unknown

Bee Happy

QUILTING BEE:
A social gathering with the
purpose of making quilts.

Life in the untamed West came with hardships, but in the spring women happily found time for needlework and socializing at quilting bees. Having spent the cold, winter months alone by the brooding fire stitching quilt tops from their stash of exchanged snippets of calico and scraps of fabric from worn-out clothing, they eagerly gathered to help each other complete the quilts. No lady wanted to be without a pieced top come spring bee time when they could again enjoy a hardy side dish of social interaction.

When the warm weather finally arrived, invitations were delivered to neighbors near and far, inviting them to join in a quilting bee. Soon all were giddy with anticipation of the big day.

They set up a large quilt frame in the refreshing sunshine as the hostess prepared a blue-ribbon supper. Benches and stools surrounded the quilt frame, and women, famished for news from the outside world, came from all walks of life to claim a spot on the benches. With a dollop of gossip and a sprinkling of giggles, their needles methodically rocked through three layers of fabric to make one harmonious quilt.

The quilt block pattern named Dresden Plate was created during the colonial revival. Other historical patterns, which were created during specific periods and handed down through generations, became a testimony to the times. Wandering Foot and Prairie Queen are from the days of the Oregon Trail, Underground Railroad is from the Civil War era, and Drunkard's Path is from the days of prohibition.

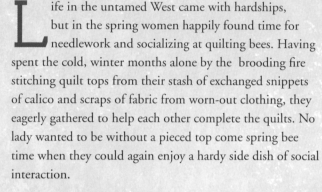

22

Mamma had Aunt Laura's silk quilt put in today and Sue is quilting on it. I am so afraid Mamma will commence work on it herself, and if she does I shall feel duty bound to put up my linen embroidery and help her. And I simply detest making and quilting quilts.

Kate Stone,
Louisiana, 1861

I have done quite a lot of canning of what is left of our fruit and vegetables and for the winter I think I shall make a quilt to keep from getting lonesome, for some of the women around here are real interested in quilting again.

From a letter from a
Minnesota woman to a
friend, 1931

After 47 years of assiduous labor Mrs. S. Lizzie Weaves, a Bridgeton, New Jersey woman, has just finished a crazy quilt of 30,075 patches.

From Kent News,
Chestertown,
Maryland, 1890

I have been looking for something to send to you, but I could not find anything that I could send in a letter but a piece of my new dress.

Hannah Shaw, 1850

23

The Quilting Bee

In fellowship sweet the ladies meet,
Their long days to invest,
Snipping, sewing, only slowing
To visit, eat or to rest.

Heads bent to task, you need not ask
If they love to quilt.
Their talented touch expresses as much,
As piece to piece it is built.

Friends try to perceive who will receive
This quilt that is stitched from the heart.
With needlework fine, the patterns
    entwined
A treasure, a true work of art.

-Author Unknown

24

We have never enjoyed ourselves with the keen zest and heartiness, in any company, that we have experienced in the old fashioned quilting party. We had but to open our eyes–to touch, to taste–to feel an exquisite delight. Of the world we knew nothing beyond the quiet village; and there we found enough to fill the measure of our capacity.

T.S. Arthur,
from The Quilting Party

Sunshine and Shadows

SUNSHINE AND SHADOWS QUILT PATTERN:
A balance of light and dark fabric squares sewn
into a radiating diamond pattern.

You are fortunate if you possess an Amish quilt, which is prized for beauty, quality, and uniqueness. Amish quilts are functional in purpose and a good example of "all things practical," yet they are beautifully pieced and intricately stitched to form quilts of heirloom quality.

Recently a few Amish have opened cottage quilt shops to help subsidize the family's farming income. Hannah, a masterful Amish quilter, owns one of these quilt shops. The small sign near the mailbox in front of her pristine, whitewashed farm reads "Hannah's Quilts and Crafts—Closed on Sundays." But don't let the quaint sign fool you. Hannah doesn't need flashing neon advertisements. Her quality craftsmanship and designs have earned her many requests for custom-made quilts from people around the nation.

It's hard to imagine, but Hannah didn't have her heart set on quilting when she was young. Although quilting is a fundamental routine for mothers and daughters in most Amish homes, Hannah wanted to be outside in the open air.

"I didn't want to stay in the house quilting, as I liked to work in the fields with my father, riding our workhorses to till the fields. But now I am glad my mother made me quilt. In those days when your parents told you to do something, you did it, and no arguments were tolerated."

Hannah further explained to me what wins the hearts of little Amish girls over to quilting. It's the fun quilting bees!

"Quilting is a great part of our Amish social life. Often when a mother is making quilts for her family's hope chest, they will set up three or four quilting frames with

26

Everything's better when shared with a friend!

quilts to be done at the same time. The children's friends and the mother's friends are all invited, which makes for a fun-filled day. You find out a lot of news from throughout the community, which we don't want to miss. So the young girls need to learn how to quilt if they want to attend these gatherings. If they can't quilt, they might get sent to the kitchen to help with the cooking. Usually this is quite the punishment as they miss out on who got married, who is having a baby, and who is moving, et cetera."

So Hannah quilted.

"My mother taught me to quilt while she was making quilts for my brothers and sisters. It's typical in the Amish community for each mother to make from three to four quilts for each child for their hope chest. Usually one is all white and one will be the solid colors with the Sunshine and Shadow pattern. This pattern was created by an Amish mother to try to use up the pieces of fabric that people would give for a baby gift when their babies were born. They are solid colors: red, greens, blues, and purples. Once one lady started doing this, it really took off, and this pattern is still being used."

The quilting bee is made even more delightful by sharing meals with those who are gathered. The Amish are not just known for their quilting skills, but also for their delicious home cooking and recipes.

"Usually a full-course meal is served at noontime plus a snack

27

of cookies and a drink in the forenoon if you get there early enough. Sandwiches, cookies, and ice cream are served as people prepare to go home, usually around three to four."

Hannah mentioned that they also have quilting bees to create specialty quilts, like the friendship quilt for a teacher who taught in their schoolhouse for many years. The mothers pieced quilt squares with their children's names embroidered on them.

They also make charity quilts when they learn of someone in need.

Since opening her quilt shop in her farmhouse in 1972, Hannah has made and seen many fine designs and quality quilts. I asked if there was one quilt in particular that was dearest to her.

"My favorite quilt is the Sunshine and Shadow quilt that my mother and sisters made for me for my hope chest when I was eighteen years old."

Recipe for Hannah's Cranberry Salad

3 (3-ounce) boxes raspberry flavored gelatin
3 cups boiling water
1 cup cold water
1 (14-ounce) can jellied cranberry sauce
2 (8-ounce) packages cream cheese, softened
1 (12-ounce) can evaporated milk

Dissolve raspberry gelatin in boiling water. Add cranberry sauce and stir until dissolved. Add cold water and cool the mixture to a semi-soft jell. Cream the evaporated milk and cream cheese together using a wire whisk, and then add to the gelatin mixture. Place in molds and refrigerate.

Hannah is refreshing, talented, and a child of God. Her story renews the spirit of the old-fashioned quilting bee. When a passion is shared, friendships are easily made.

This new friend shared one of her favorite Amish recipes, and it's now special to me. It reminds me of the many gelatin salads we set on the Thanksgiving dinner table at my grandmother's house when I was young. This dish is not only a "delicious dish to eat with a cooked meal or for a dessert for young and old," as Hannah says, but I think it is also a stylishly retro finish to a down-home comfort meal like Grandma used to make.

Fussy-Cut Treasures

FUSSY CUT:
Cutting out a specific design from printed fabric to use in a quilt block or sewing project.

What a blessing it is to own an heirloom quilt that has been passed down through the family. Like many of you, I do not have such a treasure but have purchased affordable orphaned quilts from estate sales and thrift shops. If the quilt is a bit tattered, my first objective is to mend it. I try to restore it so that it resembles its original state as much as possible. Although some quilts are worn beyond repair, with a little cutting and sewing ingenuity, they can still bring a lovely vintage touch to a space.

Ideas for Repurposed Quilts

Snip, glue, or sew a worn-out quilt to make:

- Pillow shams for the bedroom and throw pillows for the living room
- Reupholstered cushions for a small chair
- Aprons and toaster and coffeemaker covers
- Teapot cozies
- One-of-a-kind, homespun Christmas stockings, mittens, and ornaments

- Book covers for scrapbooks, guest books, and journals
- Table runners and placemats
- Unique vests
- Upholstered picture frames
- Sewing machine covers
- Cell phone and reading glass cases
- Electronic tablet totes

Preserving an Old Quilt

Lighting: Both sunlight and artificial light cause fading. Keep light levels as low as possible.

Storage: To fold a quilt, first lay it flat between two clean sheets. Then fold the quilt and the sheets in an accordion pleated fashion. This method takes extra time to accomplish, but provides the best protection for the stitching and fabric. Do not store it in plastic bags and other plastic containers, cardboard boxes, wooden trunks, chests, or drawers.

Remember: Air the quilt out once or twice a year by spreading it flat in an area with low light. Never clean with dry-cleaning chemicals.

There is no better way to make and hold onto friendships than displaying the fruits of the Spirit of God found in Galatians 5:22-23. They are love, joy, peace, patience, kindness, goodness, faithfulness, gentleness, and self-control.

Preserving an Old Friendship

Even best friends can drift apart. Marriages, careers, stress, and different phases of life can make friends unavailable. Have patience. Reconnecting in ways that don't put demands on a friend will likely rekindle the relationship. A healthy friendship can weather every stage in life.

To show you care, try giving your friend a:

• Heartfelt card
• Bouquet of flowers from your own garden
• Gift card to a coffee shop and a note that reads, "Anytime you want company, call me!"
• Small framed picture of the two of you

Marie Webster Wrote the Book

With the advent of longarm quilting machines, computerized quilting programs, and resourceful, creative people, the art of quilting is being refreshed and renewed. American quilting has emerged into a major art form and big business. Quilting magazines, books, and television shows have taken quilting from its domestic origins to a worldwide phenomenon.

Marie Webster, an avid quilter and proprietor of one of the first large-scale quilting businesses, wrote the first book about quilting in 1915. Her home in Marion, Indiana, is now a designated national historic landmark and holds the Quilting Hall of Fame.

Marie was an inspiration to women of the early twentieth century. Her original and unique applique quilt designs—mostly pastel florals—were unusual for her day. The change was welcomed, and her patterns, which were printed in magazines, were prized.

Marie's patterns are peacefully subdued in comparison to our bold, new-age quilt designs, which are limited only by the use of fabrics, embellishments, and the imagination. Velvet and corduroy, beads and sequins, bleach and ink dyes, and every conceivable material can be used to create an art quilt.

More quilts are being made at the present time—in the great cities as well as in the rural communities—than ever before, and their construction as a household occupation—and recreation—is steadily increasing in popularity. This should be a source of much satisfaction to all patriotic Americans who believe that our nation's strength lies in keeping the family hearth flame bright.

Marie Webster, from *Quilts: Their Story and How to Make Them*

33

An Artistic Adven...

ART QUILT:
The use of fabrics and embellishments to create a quilted work of art.

Using fabric as a canvas opens the way for unlimited possibilities in artistic expression. Traditional or modern, the one thing that hasn't changed over the centuries is that the quilt still tells a story of its maker.

Sometimes it's hard to try new endeavors, forge new paths, and make new friends. Fear comes from the unknown and makes us wonder if we will be accepted.

Without the pioneers of yesterday and the creative innovators of today, we'd still be quilting Nine Patches out of the same flour-sack calico. It didn't just take talent. It also took bravery and faith to walk away from the old and into the new. So it is with friendships.

Anticipating what might be is exhilarating. New-to-you quilt techniques and patterns may not turn out as planned, but the endeavor can be more fun than the finished project, and you may end up with a treasure. Again so it is with friendships!

best friends forever

ure

Color and stitch in textiles hold me captive and along with various surface design techniques I work to tell my story through my quilts. Inspiration comes from many sources...a walk in the bush, sunlight filtering through leaves in my garden, the urban landscape, a news snippet heard or just unfolding & fondling my hand-dyed fabrics.

Sue Dennis, award-winning quilter and textile artist

I can't help flying up on the wings of anticipation. It's as glorious as soaring through a sunset...almost pays for the thud.
Lucy Maud Montgomery, from Anne of Green Gables

I am fearfully and wonderfully made.
Psalm 139:14

35

An Appeal to Novelty

NOVELTY PRINT: Fabric designed with a theme, such as hobbies, animals, or holidays.

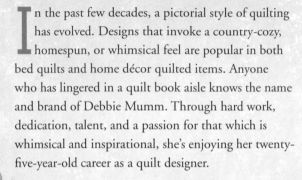

In the past few decades, a pictorial style of quilting has evolved. Designs that invoke a country-cozy, homespun, or whimsical feel are popular in both bed quilts and home décor quilted items. Anyone who has lingered in a quilt book aisle knows the name and brand of Debbie Mumm. Through hard work, dedication, talent, and a passion for that which is whimsical and inspirational, she's enjoying her twenty-five-year-old career as a quilt designer.

When Debbie talks, you get a feeling that quilting is a passion dear to her heart. Quilting is not only a creative outlet, but it's also a social endeavor. "I've made many friends through quilting. It's wonderful to know so many who 'get it.' They get that you love to touch, feel, admire, and collect fabrics. They also get what a labor of love it is to make a quilt for someone!"

All those years of hard work and success have not slowed Debbie down. Her energy is boundless, and her talent endless. Although she has a design team, Debbie follows through from concept to final production. "I get a great deal of satisfaction out of being very productive, while at the same time it's important to me to laugh and have fun with my staff and my business partners," Debbie says. "I have a very strong sense that

36

what we are doing together is a very wonderful thing."

Knowing that Debbie Mumm has designed so many quilts, I wondered if she had a favorite. She told me that, yes, she does have one. It's a quilt she made for her son and his wife for their wedding last year. It's stitched with dreams and prayers to inspire and comfort the new owners.

Debbie said, "It was fun to talk to them about what they wanted and make them part of the process. They put a lot of thought into wanting the quilt to be a timeless, family treasure. They envisioned the day that they and their children would cuddle together as a family under this quilt. They love it, and I loved making it for them."

APPLIQUÉ:
A fabric cutout that
is stitched to the top
of a quilt.

Appliqué with Aloha

Aloha! Now there is one little word with a wonderfully big attitude! "Aloha" is a greeting, a farewell, and an expression of love. The word also means a way of living life with a respectful, loving spirit.

I felt aloha as I walked into a little Hawaiian quilt shop to look for tropical fabric to make a souvenir quilt. I drooled over authentic island designs that were showcased on the walls. How could I decide what to purchase in only one short hour? I decided my best course of action was to choose a small wall quilt pattern and focus on selecting fabric for just that one project. I also vowed to allow more time at this little shop next year when I return to this land that is paradise on earth.

To save time I asked the lovely lady who was arranging patterns if there was a pineapple appliqué pattern. The pineapple is the universal symbol of welcome and friendship.

"I designed this Hawaiian pineapple," she said as she pointed to a beautiful block pattern among other gorgeous Barbara Bieraugel designer patterns.

Really? Can this really be the designer? I thought to myself.

"I'm Barbara," she said, humbly smiling at my implied question.

While we chatted I learned why Barbara moved to Hawaii, how she got started designing quilt patterns, and the story behind the quilt that is nearest to her heart, Butterflies for Amy. My new friend then went on her way to teach a class in hand-turned Hawaiian appliqué while I went on to choose fabric for my Hawaiian pineapple welcome wall quilt.

Aloha Kekahi i Kekahi
(Love one another)

When a fabric manufacturer sent Barbara a box of thirty-six beautifully colored fabrics to design a quilt pattern for them, butterflies and Amy came to mind. Butterflies are a symbol of transformation, celebration, and young love. Amy was young, a newlywed in love, and just diagnosed with leukemia.

Barbara pieced hope for Amy's recovery within the blocks of gold, green, blue, and red. She stitched each piece with love and bound the edges with faith. The quilt— filled with blessings and optimism—was completed and out the door in two and a half weeks.

That quilt has nurtured its owner for more than five years. Its story is young, but already an important one. "Over the years since 2007, this quilt pattern has been a good seller. Every time I send out a pattern, I feel that it is still sending out good vibes for Amy, who is still living on a small lake in Minnesota."

The butterfly counts not months but moments,
and has time enough.
Rabindranath Tagore

39

Wanted: Hugs and Prayers

The word "quilt" conveys warm cozy feelings. While the front and back are made from cheery fabrics lovingly chosen by the maker, the layer between is filled with batting and lining substantial enough to protect the owner from Indian attacks on the Oregon Trail and January ice storms on the prairie. Yet with tenderness, folks snuggle newborn babies and embrace the sick with them.

For the soldier who is alone in a far-off land, the elderly person who has no family to visit with, and the hospital patient with waning hope, a quilt means comfort. For the premature baby sleeping in the bassinette and the orphan with nothing to call his own, a quilt means love.

For neighbors who are sad and lonely, a quilt means someone cares. Giving a quilt is like giving a hug.

It doesn't take an award-winning quilter to make a quilt that will be cherished by someone in need. It only takes a person who wants to help another—someone who can give of themselves, do what they enjoy, and make quilts stuffed plump with hope and stitched up with a lot of love.

Search the Internet using the words "quilt charities" and many charitable opportunities will be presented. Quilt guilds, churches, hospitals, and retirement homes can also give you information on who would like to have a quilt specially made for them.

Each of you should use whatever gift you have received to serve others, as faithful stewards of God's grace in its various forms.

I Peter 4:10

to my dear friend

Perfect Piecing

PIECING:
To sew individually cut pieces of fabric together to make a pattern, sometimes called "piecework" or "patchwork."

By now you might be wondering if I have a favorite quilt story. Yes, I do, but my quilt story doesn't begin with a plan or even a desire to quilt. It starts with the necessity to win over a new friend's approval, and it takes place many years ago—when I was in college.

I met Katie Rose when a professor "pieced" us together as lab partners due to one conspicuous detail—we were the only girls amid a pack of men at the engineering college. What a blessing it was to soon learn we had more in common than wearing pink.

My treasured friend is now an aeronautical engineer. Katie is an "everything in its place" sort of woman. She has blonde hair, blue eyes, and a witty sense of humor. She would be intimidating if it weren't for her genuine warmth and love she shows to others. That's why, after just meeting her, I was hesitant to say yes when she wanted us to write our research paper at my apartment instead of her noisy dorm room. What would she think of me when she saw where I lived?

A brown plaid sofa from the second-hand shop, a wobbly rocking chair, and a reclaimed wood crate were all that could fit into the one-room apartment. The drab sleeping bag that served as a couch throw by day and bedding by night screamed "army surplus." Not much could be said of that apartment except that it was affordable. Most of my paycheck

You can never have too much fabric or too many friends

went to college tuition and books. I didn't need anything else, or so I thought until I entertained my first visitor.

Fun-loving and full of grace, my new friend didn't seem to notice the meager dwelling I could never bring myself to call "home." Yet I vowed to somehow freshen it up and make it a more presentable place before Katie's next visit.

When I left home, I took only memories and a couple boxes of clothes. Beneath the old jeans and wrinkled shirts was some fabric from one of my grandmother's visits to a flea market. A few remnants from my childhood 4-H sewing projects were also tucked in there. This confirmed that I was born with Grandma's frugal gene and the heart of a quilter. I could never throw away a scrap of fabric, and I decided that it was time to make use of them.

My first attempt at quilting was out of thrift and necessity, much like a pioneer woman on the Oregon Trail. Without instruction, pattern, or a rotary cutter, I boldly cut the fabric scraps into squares. I arranged the squares on the floor, placing them in some order of color and design. I then set quilting back two hundred years as I pieced those squares— and all the memories—together by hand with a needle and all-purpose thread. There was no batting, just an old sheet for backing. My quilt was primitive but colorful.

At Katie's next visit, her expressions of awe made it worth the late nights and sore fingers. Was it the colorful quilt and fresh flowers or the ingenuity and confidence that made such an impression?

We shared hours of laughter and a few tears while we spent late evenings and weekends studying and becoming best friends. That scrappy quilt comforted me through the toughest years of my life, years that formed who I am today.

Looking back I see that as I pieced childhood fabric scraps into a humble, utilitarian quilt, I received comfort that lasted for years. But the best piecing? That work was done by our professor!

43

In their hearts humans plan their course but the Lord establishes their steps.

Proverbs 16:9

My favorite quilt, though, is the one named Café Americano. It's pieced from the first fabric collection I designed for a major manufacturer. After twenty-five years as a professional engineer, I was given the opportunity to become what I fancied since childhood—an artist. Although I enjoyed my engineering career, I now pinch myself to see if I'm dreaming when I paint garden scenes and write what God has laid upon my heart. I'll never lose the excitement of seeing my artwork on items that make people smile, from a small garden flag on someone's porch to a large fabric collection in a quilt shop.

I see that a lifetime of learning, praying, and following God's Word leads to contentment. Although life is sometimes rough and occasionally sad, each day is joyful, peaceful, and more wondrous. I'm thankful for old friends who have lovingly encouraged me throughout the years. And I'm grateful for new friends who are put in my path.

That would be you! May you find contentment in your days, dear friend, and may all the ups and downs in your life be with a needle and thread!

Faith

44

Busy Hands & Happy Hearts

Gifts to Make the Heart Happy

Carve out time from your stressful schedule, enjoy the spirit of creativity, and make one or all three of these sweet projects. If you give them as gifts, you'll put a big smile on your friend's face and heart. I hope that you enjoy making these projects as much as I enjoyed creating them.

*Those who bring sunshine into the lives of others
cannot keep it from themselves.*
James Matthew Barrie

"I'm Going to Visit My Best Friend" Luggage Tag

"Please come for a visit" couldn't be said in a nicer way than with colorful, quilted luggage tags that can be sewn in a couple of hours.

Roll up Sewing Kit

For yourself or your frequent-flyer friend, this roll-up sewing kit can be tucked into a handbag to keep sewing or craft supplies handy. Make it in just one short day.

Kindred Hearts Tabletop Quilt

With a little quilting knowledge, you can complete this table topper in a weekend. By embroidering a personal sentiment on the center block, you create a unique gift that is sure to be cherished.

"I'm Going to Visit My Best Friend" Luggage Tag

This easy project for the beginning sewer can be made in an evening. Break out the kitschy fabric from the back of your cupboard to sew these chic and useful luggage or container tags that shout, "This package belongs to someone creative!" Use brightly colored scraps, remnants, and fat quarters or cut the tag from an old pair of jeans. Quilting is optional—fun is mandatory!

Instructions

Cut one each of fabric A, B, and interfacing C and trim top corners as shown.

Layer right sides of pieces A and B together. Place interfacing C on top.

Fold the full length of the tie strip with wrong sides together, each side meeting in the middle. Press. Fold in half again, press, and topstitch.

Tuck the entire tie between layers A and B, pinning the loose ends at the center of the top end of the tag (to be sewn in the seam).

Stitch ¼-inch seam allowances around the sides and top of the tag, leaving the bottom of the tag open.

Turn right side out.

Iron the bottom of the tag ¼ inch to the inside for a neatly hemmed appearance. Stitch around the tag close to the edge.

Quilt the tag with a pattern of your choice (optional).

Center and pin the vinyl onto the front of the tag. Stitch around the side and bottom edges.

Print and then insert a 2 x 3-inch name and address card into the vinyl pocket. A business card fits nicely too.

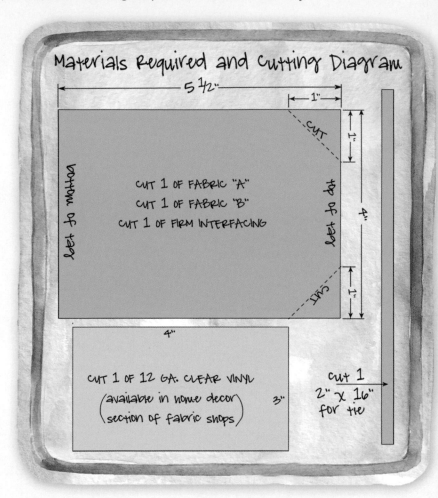

Materials Required and Cutting Diagram

CUT 1 OF FABRIC "A"
CUT 1 OF FABRIC "B"
CUT 1 OF FIRM INTERFACING

CUT 1 OF 12 GA. CLEAR VINYL (available in home decor section of fabric shops)

cut 1 2" x 16" for tie

Instructions

Layer right sides of pieces A and B together. Place quilt batting on top.

Fold each ribbon in half and tuck the ties between layers A and B. Pin the folded ends of the ribbons to the top 2 inches in from each side of the rectangle (to be sewn into the seam allowance).

Using a ¼-inch seam allowance, stitch around the rectangle, leaving an opening at the bottom.

Turn right side out to reveal the finished side of fabrics and the ribbon ties.

Iron ¼ inch to the inside of the bottom of the rectangle opening for a neatly hemmed appearance. Top stitch around the entire edge of the rectangle.

Quilt the layers with a pattern of your choice. Note that quilting is not required if you use stiffer fabric such as home décor prints or denim.

Make a yo-yo* from the round shape cut from fabric C by hand stitching a running stitch near the edge of the circle and then pulling the thread to gather the fabric into the yo-yo. Loosely stuff it with fiberfill or wadded batting. If you need more detailed instructions, see the tip below.

Turn under ¼ inch on all sides of the pocket and glasses case cut from fabric C and press. Topstitch or sew rickrack to the end of the glasses case and top of the pocket.

Pin the vinyl pocket, glasses case, fabric pocket, and yo-yo pincushion in place. Stitch the sides and bottoms of the pockets and glasses case. Hand stitch the yo-yo in place.

Pin the elastic in place, leaving enough slack to hold your implements of choice, such as thread spools. The elastic can be left flat in areas that will hold slim items such as embroidery floss or scissors. Zigzag stitch where pinned.

Fill the pockets with sewing or craft supplies. Loosely roll up the kit and tie it closed with the ribbons.

Bon voyage!

Tip: Use the Internet and books from your local library to search for new quilting patterns and learn how to embroider, create new stitches, and make the fabric yo-yos* (used for the pincushion in the roll-up sewing kit).

Roll-up Sewing Kit

This is an intermediate project and can be made in one day. When your favorite craft is at hand, traveling by plane, train, or automobile is fun. This roll-up kit can be hung on the airplane tray latch or back of a chair or rolled out on your lap. I've filled mine with embroidery supplies and a chocolate bar (or two) and traveled around the country with it. Note that children's short, blunt-nosed scissors, pins, and needles are allowed to pass through airport security.

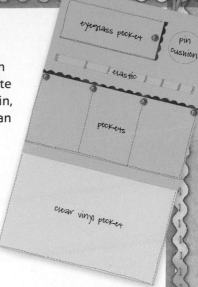

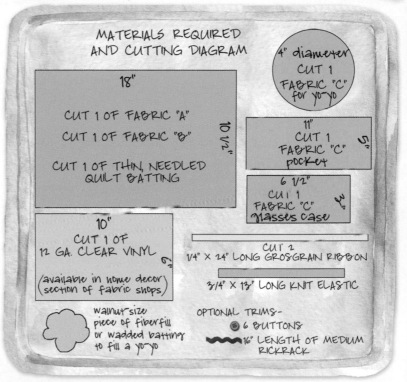

MATERIALS REQUIRED AND CUTTING DIAGRAM

4" diameter CUT 1 FABRIC "C" for yo-yo

18"
CUT 1 OF FABRIC "A"
CUT 1 OF FABRIC "B"
CUT 1 OF THIN, NEEDLED QUILT BATTING
10½"

11"
CUT 1 FABRIC "C" pocket
5"

6 ½"
CUT 1 FABRIC "C" glasses case
3"

10"
CUT 1 OF 12 GA. CLEAR VINYL
(available in home decor section of fabric shops)

CUT 2
¼" × 24" LONG GROSGRAIN RIBBON
¾" × 13" LONG KNIT ELASTIC

walnut-size piece of fiberfill or wadded batting to fill a yo-yo

OPTIONAL TRIMS-
● 6 BUTTONS
16" LENGTH OF MEDIUM RICKRACK

Kindred Hearts Tabletop Quilt

With some quilting and embroidery knowledge, this gift can be made in a weekend. Personalize the center of this quilt to make it a keepsake and reflect a treasured friendship.

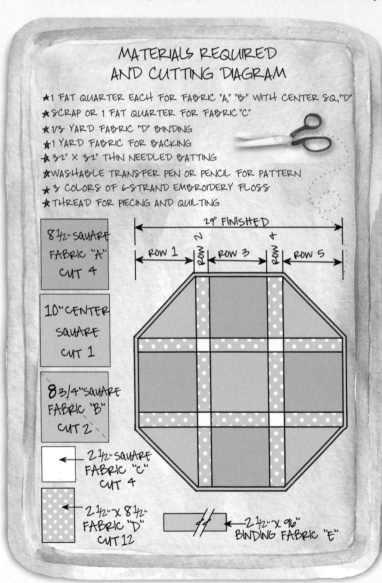

MATERIALS REQUIRED
AND CUTTING DIAGRAM

★ 1 FAT QUARTER EACH FOR FABRIC "A," "B" WITH CENTER SQ. "D"
★ SCRAP OR 1 FAT QUARTER FOR FABRIC "C"
★ 1/3 YARD FABRIC "D" BINDING
★ 1 YARD FABRIC FOR BACKING
★ 32" X 32" THIN NEEDLED BATTING
★ WASHABLE TRANSFER PEN OR PENCIL FOR PATTERN
★ 3 COLORS OF 6-STRAND EMBROIDERY FLOSS
★ THREAD FOR PIECING AND QUILTING

8 1/2" SQUARE FABRIC "A" CUT 4

10" CENTER SQUARE CUT 1

8 3/4" SQUARE FABRIC "B" CUT 2

2 1/2" SQUARE FABRIC "C" CUT 4

2 1/2" X 8 1/2" FABRIC "D" CUT 12

2 1/2" X 96" BINDING FABRIC "E"

29" FINISHED — ROW 1, ROW 2, ROW 3, ROW 4, ROW 5

Instructions

Note: Use ¼-inch seam allowances on all seams. Use fabric and embroidery floss colors of your choice.

Cut the 10-inch square center block, which is larger than required to allow for embroidering. Using a copy machine or computer scanner, enlarge the embroidery pattern 200 percent, making sure it measures 6½ inches in diameter.

Center and transfer the embroidery pattern onto the fabric block using these three steps. First, tape the pattern to a sunny window. Next, center and tape the fabric over the pattern. Finally, trace the pattern onto the fabric using a water-soluble, fabric marking pen.

Embroider the vine and words with 3 strands of floss. Use a color that will show up well on the fabric. Embroider the leaves using a lazy daisy stitch and then the flowers (dots) by making French knots.

Cut out two hearts (or more if you have a group of friends). If you would like, embroider your initials and those of your friend(s) on the hearts. Blanket stitch the hearts onto the block.

Trim the center block to an 8½-inch square, centering the embroidered design. Cut the rest of the fabric pieces. Cut the two fabric B squares in half diagonally as shown by the dashed line. Cut and stitch together enough 2½-inch wide pieces of fabric E to make a 96-inch long binding strip.

Assemble row 1 pieces as shown. Then assemble row 2 and continue through row 5.

Sew row 1 to row 2. Sew row 2 to row 3 and continue until the quilt top is assembled.

Layer backing, batting, and the quilt top. Quilt as desired. Trim all edges to form a neat octagon.

Fold and press binding in half. Stitch the raw edges of the binding to the edge of the quilt, right side to right side. Turn binding and hand stitch to the back of the quilt.

Make a permanent label with your name, date, and why you made the quilt. Attach it to the back of the quilt top.

6½"
(AFTER ENLARGED 200%)

kindred hearts

HEART PATTERN
(ENLARGE 200%)

EMBROIDERY PATTERN
(ENLARGE 200%)

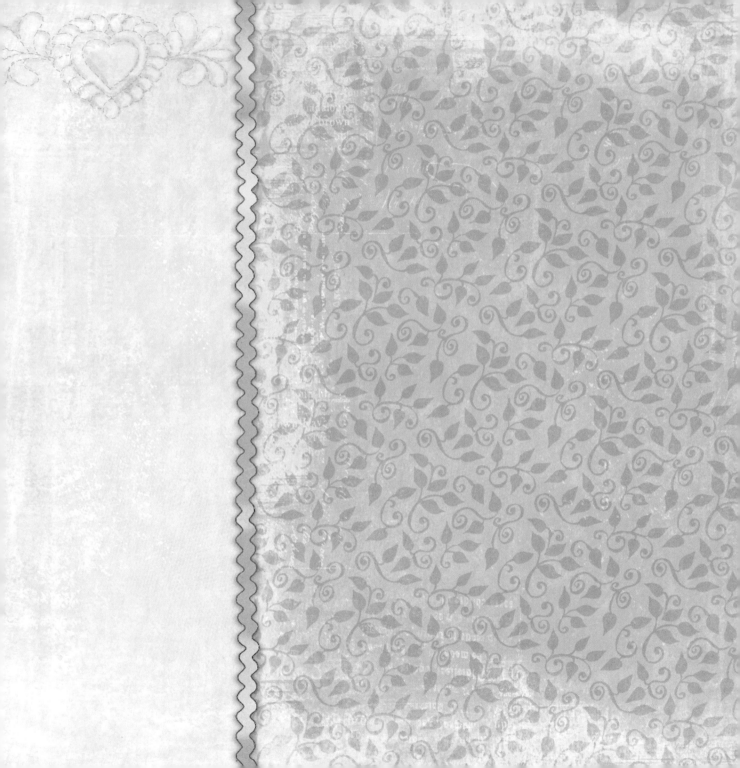